THE

HORARY ASTROLOGY

Kim Farnell

.

CONTENTS

INTRODUCTION

Horary astrology is based on the idea that every moment of time has its own quality. A chart can be cast for the birth of a person, nation, business, institution or idea and that chart describes what it is cast for. Horary astrology assumes that the answer to a question lies in the moment it is asked.

Personal details, such as date, place and time of birth are not needed. There is no need for a birth chart when using horary astrology. It is a highly structured form of astrology with strict rules, but once you are competent it is the fastest and easiest way of using astrology to answer a specific question.

A horary chart shows the background of your question, what is happening at present in relation to the question, and what is likely to happen if you let nature run its course. Although it describes the likely outcome of a situation, this doesn't mean you have no control over what is going to happen. The chart reflects the circumstances at the time of asking the question. By making changes you can change the outcome.

Horary astrology differs from modern natal astrology in a number of ways. It relies on traditional techniques that are no longer used in natal astrology and does not (usually) use the modern planets Neptune, Uranus and Pluto. It also only uses the major aspects.

Horary astrology only considers the parts of the chart relevant to the question. Modern astrology books tend to focus on the principles of astrological symbolism. With horary astrology you need to be specific about what a planet in a certain position means. The other planets can supply supporting information, but they won't answer the question.

Here is a famous horary cast by famous horary astrologer William Lilly in the seventeenth century. You may be unfamiliar with some of the terminology used, but it will give you an idea of how to approach a horary chart and you can return to it when you have read the remainder of the book. The English has been modernised for ease of reading.

Original question: *In the year 1643, his majesty's army being then rampant, several reports were given out, that his majesty had taken Cambridge, etc. A well-affected person enquired of me if the news were true or false?*

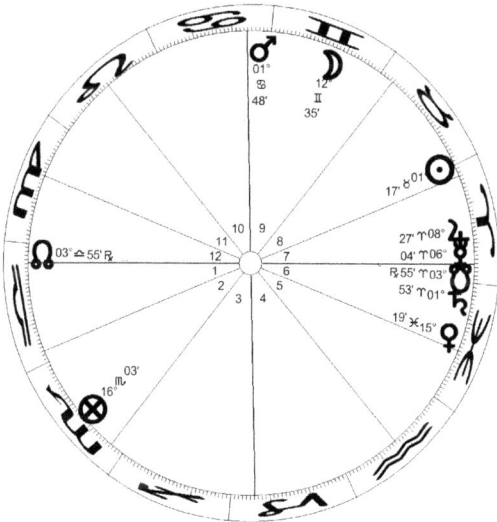

Lilly concluded that the rumour was false based on the following:

The angles (1st, 7th, 4th and 10th house cusps) are all in cardinal signs, and Mars is on the cusp of the 10th house and Saturn on the cusp of the 7th house. Both Saturn and Mars are *malefics* (bad planets) so this suggests the rumour is false.

The Moon is in a cadent house and in Gemini. A cadent house is weak and the Moon is not strong in Gemini. This again suggests a false rumour.

The North Node is on the ascendant which is positive for Parliament (in opposition to the King) because the 1st

3

house represents Parliament, and the ascendant is ruled by Venus which is exalted. This puts Parliament in a strong position. Conversely, Mars rules the 7th house and so the enemy of Parliament, the King. Mars is debilitated by being in the sign of his fall and is making a square to Saturn. This square suggests division and treason on the part of Parliament's enemies. In addition, the Moon is separating from a sextile to Jupiter and approaching a trine with Venus, showing that Parliament would gain the most. Lilly later found out that his conclusions were correct and the rumour was untrue.

THE QUESTION

The time used for a horary chart is the moment when the question is clear in your head. If you are answering someone else's question, your chart is cast for when YOU understand the question and for your location. The place you cast the chart for is where YOU are when you understand the question, regardless of the location of the person who has sent it to you.

A horary chart answers the question you actually asked rather than the question you *thought* you were asking, so you need to be careful it's phrased properly.

For example, if you ask *Should I marry John?* the word *should* implies that you're asking whether it would be a good idea or not. *Will I marry John?* suggests you're asking whether a wedding is likely to take place.

The easiest questions to answer are those that are phrased in a way that they can be answered by yes or no. If the answer is no, the chart can show ways of improving the situation.

You can ask more complex questions but the hardest ones to try and answer are those that involve a choice between two different things: *Should I do this thing or that thing?* It's better to rephrase the question so it can be answered with a yes or no: *If I do this thing, will it be successful?*

Each question should only be asked once unless circumstances have changed drastically. If you don't like the answer you get, you can't ask the same question again in the hope of a better answer.

This is why horary is unsuitable for asking who is going to win the Cup Final or become the next Prime Minister. You have no way of knowing when the question was first asked.

The lifespan of a question is usually about three months, assuming nothing changes drastically in the meantime. Because of this, horary doesn't work very well for questions such as *Will I ever marry?* but is better for questions such as *Am I likely to get married in the next six weeks?*

The person who asks the question is known as the *querent*.

The matter being asked about is known as the *quesited*.

The person who asks the question is signified by the planet that rules the ascendant. The first house of the chart and the Moon describes the querent and their circumstances, the movement of events or their motivation for asking the question.

The matter asked about is represented by the house that rule that matter and signified by the planet that rules that house.(Planets that fall in the house may offer further information.)

The answer to the question is supplied by the relationship between the signifying planets. If they relate well, the matter goes smoothly. If they relate badly, things won't go as you'd hoped.

CONSIDERATIONS

Once you have cast your chart, you need to consider whether it's radical or not—in other words whether it can give you a clear answer to your question. These *considerations against judgement* are matters to consider rather than rules against reading the chart. For example, it may be that circumstances will change and therefore the nature of the question might change. Or the person asking the question might not be honest and their motives may be different to how they are presented.

Planetary hour: The ruler of the hour should be of the same triplicity or nature as the ruler of the ascendant (rarely used today).

To find the planetary hour, divide the time between sunrise and sunset into 12 equal parts. Take the ruler of that day of the week: Sunday/Sun; Monday/Moon; Tuesday/Mars; Wednesday/Mercury; Thursday/Jupiter; Friday/Venus and Saturday/Saturn. The first hour is ruled by the planet ruling the day. The succeeding hours are ruled by the planets in the following order: Saturn, Jupiter, Mars, Sun, Venus, Mercury and Moon. Similarly, the time between sunset and the following sunrise is divided into twelve equal parts to give the night planetary hours.

The ascendant must not be too early (0°-3°). An ascendant in very early degrees suggests that it is too early to judge.

The ascendant must not be too late (27°-30°). This suggests the querent may already know the answer.

The ascendant and the planet in the ascendant must describe the querent.

The Moon must not be square or in opposition to the ruler of the 7th house.

The Moon must not lie in the via combusta.
    Definitions of the via combusta vary. In modern terms it is described as 15° Libra to 15° Scorpio. However, traditionally the area is much smaller—about 19° Libra to 3° Scorpio.

The Moon must not be void of course—where it perfects no aspect to another planet before leaving the sign it is in, therefore generally in late degrees of a sign. It suggests that the activity planned will come to nothing.

The cusp of the seventh house and its lord must not be afflicted. In horary questions not related to matters ruled by the seventh house, the descendant and its ruler signify the astrologer. Therefore, this suggests that the astrologer may not be able to answer the question.

Saturn should not be on the ascendant or in the first house, especially if retrograde (as above).

Saturn should not be in the seventh house (as above).

First house ruler should not be combust (within 7½ degrees of the Sun).

There should not be an equal number of fortunate and unfortunate factors, meaning the answer is unclear.

So the process is:

- Define your question
- Calculate the chart using a quadrant house system such as Regiomontanus or Placidus.
- Decide whether you can and should judge this chart.
- Isolate the parts of the chart you need to answer your question.

PLANETS

The most important part of horary astrology is to correctly assign the appropriate planets to the characters and events in the question. These planets are called *significators* because they signify the relevant individuals or incidents. The answer to a horary question is found by looking at the condition and movement of the significators.

The person who asks the question is called the *querent*. The querent is always primarily signified by the planet that rules the ascendant. The condition of the 1st house, any planets in the 1st house, and the Moon also help to describe the querent's situation.

The matter asked about is called the *quesited*. It is described by the house that naturally governs that matter and signified by the planet that rules the cusp of that house. Other planets located in that house offer further descriptive information.

The planets are often regarded as literal representatives of the events and characters in the querent's life. They can give physical descriptions and behavioural characteristics of another person represented by that planet.

The Moon is a general significator for the whole situation. It may help to represent the querent, describe surrounding circumstances, or it could describe the movement of events or related issues that may not be immediately apparent.

For example, with the question *Is my husband going to leave me?* the querent is represented by the planet that rules the ascendant. If Libra rises, the significator will be Venus. In addition to the position and condition of Venus, you will also need to consider the details that are added by planets in the first house, or those that are in close contact with Venus. In this chart, Aries will be descending and since the querent's question concerns her husband, who falls under the rulership of the 7th house, Mars is taken as the significator for the quesited. The position and condition of Mars will add detail, as will any additional planet in the 7th house.

As the Moon acts as a general significator, its relationship with the other planets and significators will refine the judgement.

Each planet can represent certain things outright, this is called *natural* rulership. This can be helpful when, for example, the same planet rules both the querent and the quesited. You can also look at any planet that is in the house that signifies the issue.

Planetary strength

Jupiter and Venus are the gre*ater and lesser benefics* and are naturally fortunate. Saturn and Mars are the *greater and lesser malefics* and naturally unfortunate. This may change according to the chart. For example, if Jupiter rules the 8th house of death it may be unfortunate.

The planetary ruler modifies the way in which another planet in that sign expresses its energy. A planet in a sign has to conform to the energy of its ruler. This suits some planets and not others. Sometimes the planet is in the sign it also rules and can express its energy clearly.

Dignities are measurements of a planet's strength. *Rulership* is the first and main dignity. The other *essential* dignities (due to the planet's position in the zodiac) are *exaltation*, *triplicity*, *term* and *face*. The more dignity a planet has, the stronger it is.

The opposite to dignity is *debility*; this is a measurement of weakness. The debilities are *detriment*, which is opposite to rulership, and *fall*, which is opposite to exaltation.

The strength of the planets helps decide whether the answer to the question is yes or no.

Rulership: Apart from the Sun and Moon, each planet rules one sign by day and one by night. A day chart is when the Sun is above the horizon (in houses 7 to 12). This is its strongest position. Day rulerships are more active and relate to masculinity, being active, direct and expressive. Night rulerships are more passive in nature and relate to femininity, being responsive and indirect. For example, Mars in Aries expresses itself in an active and direct manner whilst the Mars in Scorpio's energy is released slowly, deliberately and with cold control. Although in modern astrology Mars and Aries are often treated in the same way, they are very different in horary astrology.

Planets in rulership are strong. The planet is at home, able to make decisions and feels comfortable.

In modern natal astrology, the outer planets are given rulerships of some signs—Uranus for Aquarius, Neptune for Pisces and Pluto for Scorpio. The outer planets are generally not used in horary. The exception to this is when they clearly rule the matter in hand. For example, a question about nuclear power is related to Pluto.

A practical reason to maintain the traditional sign rulerships in horary is that the outer planets tend to represent social or political influences and their slow movement fails to convey personal influence in the way the quicker moving visible planets are able to.

Using the traditional rulerships means that issues that are commonly associated with the outer planets in modern natal astrology have to be re-allocated to the planet that originally rules them. For example, drugs and alcohol are traditionally associated with Mars whereas in modern astrology they are often associated with Neptune. Similarly, Uranus represents electricity.

Exaltation: Although the planet is exalted in the whole sign, the exact degree of exaltation is where its strongest. A planet in exaltation is strengthened. It is like a welcomed guest with things being done for it, comfortable but not totally at home. The strength of the planet is augmented and its virtues are magnified. It is only slightly less favourably placed than when it is in its own sign.

Triplicity: The rulers change depending on whether the chart is a day or night chart. A planet in its own triplicity is in a place that suits it, although it hasn't made any effort to get there. It acts like a neighbour popping around for coffee in a familiar, relaxed environment.

Term: The Sun and Moon don't rule any terms. Mars and Saturn rule the final terms of every sign. A planet in its own term is slightly strengthened. It is not in a position of power but acts like an acquaintance invited into your home. The planet is in a situation of temporary strength, although it might not otherwise suit the sign it is in.

Face: Faces are also known as *decanates* or *decans*. A planet in its own face is slightly fortunate, accepted, but not totally comfortable. The faces represent worry or concern about matters related to the planet in question.

Detriment: This is a planet's weakest position and where it is harmed or damaged. The planet functions at a disadvantage. It cannot operate at full strength and needs to adhere to rules.

Fall: A planet in fall is severely weakened and cannot express itself properly.

A planet with no essential dignity is weakened and called *peregrine*. A peregrine planet is a drifter; one that is not attached to the place it is in and it is weakened.

Once you have found each planet's position on the table of dignities you can give it points according to which dignities or debilities it has. This makes it easy to compare the relative strengths of the planets.

Sign	Exaltation	Triplicity	Term	Face	Detriment	Fall
+5	+4	+3	+2	+1	-5	-4

Joy

Each of the planets *joys* or *rejoices* in one of the houses and each house is co-signified by one of the signs and planets. A planet in its house of joy is strengthened and its influence is emphasised. It is the place that the planet most enjoys being in and is most suited to its natural expression. The 2nd, 4th, 7th, 8th and 10th houses don't have a planet that rejoices in them. Planetary joys add an emphasis to the planet. For example, Venus rejoices in the 5th house of love affairs and procreation and its influence is strengthened by its location in a house that is fundamentally suitable to its character.

Mercury 1st house; Moon 3rd; Venus 5th; Mars 6th; Sun 9th; Jupiter 11th; Saturn 12th

Accidental dignity

Accidental dignity occurs when a planet falls in a position unrelated to its zodiacal position, in which it is more powerful. An accidental dignity is like being in the right place at the right time. Conversely, an accidental debility denotes problems.

Sign	Ruler	Exalted	Trip. D/N	Terms (up to)					Faces (up to 10, 20, 30)			Det.	Fall
♈	♂ (d)	☉ 19	☉/♃	♃ 6	♀ 14	☿ 21	♂ 26	♄ 30	♂	☉	♀	♀	♄
♉	♀ (n)	☽ 3	♀/☽	♀ 8	☿ 15	♃ 22	♄ 26	♂ 30	☿	☽	♄	♂	
♊	☿ (d)	☊ 3	♄/☿	☿ 7	♃ 14	♀ 21	♄ 25	♂ 30	♃	♂	☉	♃	
♋	☽	♃ 15	♂/♂	♂ 6	♃ 13	20 ♀	27 ♄	☿ 30	♀	☿	☽	♄	♂
♌	☉		☉/♃	♄ 6	☿ 13	♀ 19	♃ 25	♂ 30	♄	♃	♂	♄	
♍	☿ (n)	☿ 15	♀/☽	☿ 7	♀ 13	♃ 18	♄ 24	♂ 30	☉	♀	☿	♃	♀
♎	♀ (d)	♄ 21	♄/☿	♄ 6	♀ 11	♃ 19	☿ 24	♂ 30	☽	♄	♃	♂	☉
♏	♂ (n)		♂/♂	♂ 6	♃ 14	♀ 21	☿ 27	♄ 30	♂	☉	♀	♀	☽
♐	♃ (d)	☋ 3	☉/♃	♃ 8	♀ 14	☿ 19	♄ 25	♂ 30	☿	☽	♄	☿	
♑	♄ (n)	♂ 28	♀/☽	♀ 6	☿ 12	♃ 19	♂ 25	♄ 30	♃	♂	♄	☽	♃
♒	♄ (d)		♄/☿	♄ 6	☿ 12	♀ 20	♃ 25	♂ 30	♀	☿	☽	☉	
♓	♃ (n)	♀ 27	♂/♂	♀ 8	♃ 14	☿ 20	♂ 26	♄ 30	♄	♃	♂	☿	☿

Accidental dignities

In the midheaven or ascendant	+5
In the 7th, 4th and 11th houses	+4
In the 2nd and 5th	+3
In the 9th	+2
In the 3rd house	+1
Direct (doesn't apply to Sun and Moon)	+4
Faster than average daily motion	+2
Saturn, Mars, Jupiter oriental (cusp of tenth house westward to fourth via the descendant is occidental, the opposite half is oriental. There are other definitions).	+2
Mercury, Venus occidental	+2
The Moon occidental, or increasing in light	+2
Free from combustion and the Sun's rays	+5
Cazimi (less than 17' from the Sun	+5
Partile (same degree) conjunction Jupiter or Venus	+5
Partile conjunction with North Node	+4
Partile trine with Jupiter or Venus	+4
Partile sextile with Jupiter or Venus	+3
Partile conjunction with Regulus (29°53' Leo)	+6
Partile conjunction with Spica (23° 50' Libra)	+5

Accidental deblities

In the 12th house	-5
In the 8th and 6th	-2
Retrograde	-5
Slower than average daily motion	-2
Saturn, Jupiter, Mars occidental	-2
Moon decreasing in light	-2
Combust the Sun (between 17 and 8.5°)	-5
Under the Sun's beams (between 8.5° and 17° of Sun	-4
Partile conjunction with South Node	-4
Besieged between Saturn and Mars	-5
Partile opposition of Saturn or Mars	-4
Partile square of Saturn or Mars	-3
Within 5° of Caput Agol (26°10' Taurus)	-5

Planet	Avg. Daily M
Sun	0°59'
Moon	13°11'
Mercury	1°23'
Venus	1°12'
Mars	0°31'
Jupiter	0°05'
Saturn	0°02'

18

Planets and their rulerships

☽

The Moon is associated with night and is a *luminary*, or light bringer. The Moon is particularly important when deciding timing, and its speed needs to be taken into account. The Moon is always the co-ruler of the querent and question and may also symbolise the mother or a woman involved in the issue. The Moon is neither fortunate or unfortunate but takes on a positive or negative meaning according her placement in the chart and how she connects with the other planets. When badly placed she signifies someone who dislikes work and is idle.

Rules: Emotions, intuition, home, women, lost objects, short trips, changes, queens and female nobility, mother, general public, travellers, those who make a living from the sea (sailors, fishermen, fishmongers), those who work with liquids (barmen), postmen, cleaners, midwives, nurses, drunkards, fugitives.

Enemy planets: Saturn and Mars.
Friendly planets: Jupiter, Sun, Venus and Mercury.
Day: Monday daytime and Thursday night.
Age: Infancy until seven years of age.
Appearance: Pale complexion, round face, grey eyes, fleshy and plump body, short fleshy hands.
Colour: Silver, white, pale green, and pale yellow.
Creatures: All who use the water, goose, swan, duck, shellfish, dog, frog, goat, tortoise, cat, mouse, rat.
Metal: Silver.
Places: Fountains, field, ports, roads, rivers, deserts,

pools, fishponds, bogs, brooks, docks, wharves.

Body parts: Brain, left eye of a man and right eye of a woman, reproductive system.

Diseases: Migraine, vertigo, colic, diseases in the bladder, testicles and left side, and in the liver of women, genitals, menstrual disorders, sciatica, coughs, convulsions, measles.

⊙

The Sun is a luminary, a masculine planet and associated with the daytime. The Sun may be considered a co-ruler of the querent if he is a man. He also signifies the person of authority or from whom a favour is desired.

Rules: Monarchs, all nobles, those in office or command, coiners, bankers, goldsmiths, tyrants, usurpers, constables, all who bear any authority, men, employers, officials, father, magistrates.

Enemy planet: Saturn.
Friendly planets: Jupiter, Mars, Venus, Mercury, Moon.
Day: Sunday daytime and Wednesday night.
Direction: East.
Appearance: Middle sized, strong and portly, stately gait, tanned complexion, light and frizzy or curly hair, large, full hazel eyes, broad forehead.
Colour: Yellow (also scarlet and purple).
Creatures: Stately, wild, bold, strong animals, horse.
Metal: Gold.
Places: Palaces, courts, houses, all magnificent buildings, halls, dining rooms.
Body parts: The heart, brain and right eye in men and left eye in women.
Diseases: Heart palpitations, eye problems, cramps, giddiness, diseases of the mouth and brain, catarrh, fever.

☿

Mercury is neither masculine or feminine, being strongly influenced by any planet it connects to.

Rules: News, speech, trade, business, contracts, neighbours, young people, offices, letters, the media, short journeys, cars, astrologers, mathematicians, secretaries, merchants, advocates, teachers, accountants, clerks, solicitors, thieves, couriers, computer operators.

Enemy planets: Mars, Sun and Moon.
Friendly planets: Jupiter, Venus and Saturn.
Day: Wednesday daytime and Saturday night.
Direction: Northern.
Age: From 7 to 14.
Appearance: Colourless face, high forehead, long face and nose, thin lips, dull eyes, dark hair, long hands and fingers, tall, upright, spare body.
Colour: Mixed colours.
Creatures: Melodious birds, parrot, dog, and those that are of quick sense, ingenious, inconstant, swift, and easily domesticated, fox, squirrel, spider, ant.
Metals: Quicksilver, tin.
Places: Schools, tennis courts, fairs, markets, bowling alleys, shop, hall in a house, study, library.
Body parts: Brain, tongue, and left ear.
Diseases: Vertigo, lethargy, madness, diseases of the brain, stammering, defects of memory, hoarseness, dry cough, gout.

♀

Venus is the *lesser benefic* and a feminine planet. She is associated with all matters connected with affection, beauty, love, lovers and good deeds. She is the planet of luxury, enjoyment and amusement.

Rules: Musicians, game players, embroiderers, jewellers, drapers, perfumers, artists, anyone in the beauty industry, women, wives, mothers, painters, upholsterers, creativity, gifts, money, marriage, decorators.

Enemy planet: Saturn.
Friendly planets: Jupiter, Mars, Sun, Mercury and Moon.
Day: Friday daytime and Monday night.
Direction: Southern.
Age: From 14 to 22.
Appearance: Light, smooth hair, fair complexion, dark eyes, round face, dimple, light and nimble.
Colour: Blue tending to white or white.
Creatures: Dog, rabbit, sheep, goat, bull, calf.
Metals: Copper and brass.
Places: Beds and bedrooms, dining rooms, places where dancing takes place, gardens, fountains, wardrobes, restaurants, cafes, places of pleasure.
Body parts: Kidneys, backbone, private parts.
Diseases: Kidney and bladder disease, venereal disease, diabetes, any condition caused by over-indulgence.

♂

Mars is the *lesser malefic* and is a masculine planet.

Rules: Passion, action, accidents, sex, weapons, quarrels, injury, anger, drugs, poison, courage, boldness, crime, violence, conquerors, usurpers, tyrants, soldiers, physicians, chemists, surgeons, butchers, gunners, watchmakers, barbers, all who use iron tools, carpenters, cooks, tailors, smiths, bakers. When in a difficult position he denotes thieves, bailiffs, murderers, jailers.

Enemy planet: Moon.
Friendly planets: Saturn, Jupiter, Sun, Venus and Mercury.
Day: Tuesday daytime and Friday night.
Direction: Western.
Age: From 22 to 45.
Appearance: Red haired, red face, fiery eyes, short, strong and big boned, seldom fat.
Colour: Red, yellow or saffron.
Creatures: All beasts that are ravenous and bold, birds of prey.
Metals: Iron, steel, arsenic.
Places: All places related to fire and blood, such as slaughter houses, furnaces, smiths shops, butchers.
Body parts: Back, veins, gallbladder.
Diseases: Fever, migraine, shingles, fistulas, kidney stones, jaundice, hepatitis.

4

Jupiter is the *greater benefic* and is a masculine planet

Rules: Charity, fidelity, integrity, extravagance, judges, councillors, religious workers, priests, chancellors, someone wise and experienced, senators, lawyers, scholars, students, opportunity, gambling, speculation, higher education, prophecy, foreigners, horse racing, advertising, the wealthy.

Enemy planet: Mars.
Friendly planets: Saturn, Sun, Venus, Mercury and Moon.
Day: Thursday daytime and Sunday night.
Direction: North and north east.
Age: Middle age.
Appearance: Upright straight tall stature, ruddy complexion, oval face, plump, high forehead, soft hair, large grey eyes, brown hair, short neck.
Colour: Green blue, purple, green and a mixed yellow
Creatures: Large beasts in general, bees.
Metals: Tin and pewter.
Places: Churches and other religious buildings, gardens, courts, wardrobes, palaces.
Body parts: Liver.
Diseases: Infirmities of the liver, pleurisy, inflammation of the lungs, infirmities in the left ear, heart palpitations, cramps, pains in the back.

♄

Saturn is the *greater malefic* and is a masculine planet.

Rules: Duty, burdens, old people, debt, poverty, loss, death, restrictions, sailors, plumbers, labourers, beggars, undertakers, bricklayers, scavengers, miners, gardeners, herdsmen, father, grandfather.

Enemy planet: Jupiter, Sun and Mercury.
Friendly planets: Mars, Venus and Moon.
Day: Saturday daytime and Tuesday night.
Direction: East.
Age: Old age.
Appearance: Middle stature, pale, swarthy, or muddy, small black eyes, broad forehead, black or very dark hair, large ears, low eyebrows, thick lips, and nose, thin beard, heavy countenance, large shoulders, thin thighs.
Colour: Black, dark brown.
Creatures: Creatures that creep, cat, hare, mouse, dog, serpent, toad.
Metals: Lead.
Places: Deserts, woods, hidden valleys, caves, holes, churchyards, ruined buildings, coal pits, sinks, dirty places, wells, offices.
Body parts: Spleen.
Diseases: Epilepsy, fistulas, depression, aches and colds in the joints, deafness, toothache, pains in the bones, in the bladder, gout, catarrh.

HOUSES

The first house always represents the person asking the question, or querent. The other house is chosen because of its association with the question. For example, the 10th house is used for career questions. The planets that rule the cusps of the relevant houses supply the answer to the question.

A 5° orb of influence precedes the cusps of the houses. In other words, if the ascendant is 17° Capricorn and a planet is at 15° Capricorn, it is considered to be in the first house. The cusp is the most powerful point of the house's influence and any planet close to a cusp highlights the affairs of that house. This assumes that the planet in question is in the same sign as the cusp.

The nature of the houses

The houses are not all equal in strength and power.

Angular houses begin with the angles. When a planet is in an angular house, it performs more powerfully. Whatever it represents will show its force in a swift and dynamic fashion. If a planet is located in an angular house, it is more forceful in its effects than it would be in a cadent house. Any planet in conjunction with an angle will have a marked influence that resonates throughout the chart and colours its overall meaning. Angular planets are powerful, so the people or matters that they signify are strong and attract a lot of attention. The further the distance between a planet and the angles the less potency it possesses.

The *succedent* houses are so-named because the planets within them succeed by the daily movement of the heavens to the cardinal position. Succedent placements are of mediocre strength.

The word *cadent* means fallen. A planet in a cadent house has been carried by the daily movement away from the cardinal position, symbolising something that has moved from a position of power into a condition of weakness, or a fall from grace.

The type of house a planet falls in is also important for matters of timing. Angular, planets bring a swift result, succedent planets perform more slowly and cadent planets are so ineffective that often they don't perform at all or they take a very long time.

Each house governs a variety of related matters and people. As we choose our significators by working out which house is most closely associated with our question, it's important to have a detailed knowledge of house rulership.

First house: Querent and their state of mind, appearance, temperament and body.

Second house: Personal possession which is movable, lost object. Money, wealth, profit and gain, income and loss and bank account. Lawyer and witnesses in a court case.

Third house: Brothers and sisters, relations, neighbours, short journeys, messengers, rumours, newspapers, reporters, writing, letters, post offices, telephone calls, and cars.

Fourth house: Ancestry, inheritance and father, real estate, buildings, end of anything and treasures hidden in the ground.

Fifth house: Pregnancy, children, enjoyment and entertainment, games, gambling, speculation, pubs and bars. Romance but not love affairs, sex and creative pursuits.

Sixth house: Illness, healing, service, preoccupation with work, trade and merchandise, employees, lodgers, tenants, computers. Pets and small animals.

Seventh house: All forms of partnership, love affairs, love, marriage, open enemies, competition, divorce, lawsuits, other party in a court case, contracts, thieves, fugitives and runaways.

Eighth house: Death, other people's money, wills, legacies, dowry, undertakers.

Ninth house: Universities, religion, clergy, foreign lands and languages, long journeys, journeys of significance, foreign trade, explorers, dreams, visions, legal entities, legalising procedures (such as marriage ceremonies), ritual, standards and rules.

Tenth house: Royalty and those held in esteem, judges, magistrates, presidents, commanders, captains and prime ministers, profession or trade, authority, dignity of office, and victory, social standing, government, law enforcement officers.

Eleventh house: Friends, hope, wishes, trust, confidence, ambition and praise. Societies and their members. Benefactors,

Twelfth house: Secret enemies, hidden matters, family scandals, sorrow and undoing, witches and informers, and afflictions. Large institutions like hospitals and prisons. Solitude, mysticism, monks, nuns, and sleep. Large animals. What you secretly fear. Malicious rumours, gossip. Crime, lying.

Places

The significator for a missing object in an angular house shows it is near its owner, and suggests a quick recovery. It is likely to be indoors and near the querent.

The significator for a missing object in a succedent houses shows it is some way off but not too far. It could also indicate that it is to the right.

The significator for a missing object in a cadent house shows it is some distance away from the querent. It could be to the left.

The houses represent directions as follows:

1: East	2: E-N-E	3:	N-N-E
4: North	5: N-N-W	6:	W-N-W
7: West	8: W-S-W	9:	S-S-W
10: South	11:S-S-E	12:	E-S-E

Time

The precise time units you use will depend on the nature of the question. Fixed signs give the longest time-unit, cardinal the shortest and mutable the middle unit. This could be hours, days and weeks or days, weeks and months (for example). The 1st house often indicates the present or today, the 2nd house the immediate future or tomorrow, the 4th house the end of the matter and the 12th house yesterday or the distant past.

Turning the houses

The houses are not all equal in strength and when someone asks a question about another person, you may find it necessary to skip around the chart to derive the house suitable to that person inquired about. In that case, the house that represents them in the chart becomes their first house. For example, if you were asking a question about your sister's job, the third house represents her in the chart. Her job is represented by the tenth house from the third or 12th house of the chart.

The precise house depends on the quesited's (the person/thing asked about) relationship to the querent. For example, for a question about your paternal grandmother, you take the 4th house for your father and then the 10th from the 4th for your father's mother.

Similarly, if you were considering going into business with a partner, you would be the querent and described by the 1st house and signified by the planet that rules the 1st house. Your potential partner would be described by the 7th house and signified by the planet that rules the 7th house. The 2nd house of the chart will describe your own financial situation, but the 8th house could be used as a turned 2nd house to describe your partner's financial situation.

It may not always be necessary to turn the chart. Your neighbour's plumber remains a plumber whether they are currently working for your neighbour or not. They would therefore fall under the 6th house. If in doubt, look at both places and see if one significator obviously matches the person better than the other.

SIGNS

The planet used to represent the question the one that rules the sign at the start of the house connected with that issue.

Some signs take longer than others to rise on the eastern horizon and so remain on the ascendant longer than others. On average, a sign takes two hours to rise. Signs of *long ascension* take longer: Cancer, Leo, Virgo, Libra, Aquarius, Sagittarius. Signs of *short ascension* take less time: Capricorn, Aquarius, Pisces, Aries, Taurus, Gemini.

The Sun and Moon each rule one sign and the other planets rule one sign in the daytime and another at night. (In modern astrology the distinction between day and night rulers is ignored and the outer planets are given rulerships of signs: Uranus for Aquarius, Neptune for Pisces and Pluto for Scorpio.)

The daytime expression of a planet is active, direct and expressive whereas its night time expression is responsive, indirect and impressive. A planet is most at home when in a sign it rules.

Each zodiac sign belongs to a number of groups and the meanings of these groups combined act together to form the sign's meaning.

Polarity

Masculine signs tend to be active whereas feminine signs tend to be acted upon. In modern astrology these are often known as *positive* and *negative*. Masculine signs are associated with the daytime and feminine signs with the night.

Season

Each sign is associated with a season of the year. Using the seasonal qualities accounts for the differences in expression between signs of the same element. All fire signs are hot and dry. However, the addition of the elemental qualities of the seasons results in differences between the fire signs. For example, Leo being the midsummer sign gets a double dose of hot and dry and is the pure fire sign, but Aries as a spring sign is wetter.

Element

The four elements are the main building blocks of life and are air, earth, fire and water.

Fire signs put out energy, act quickly and are dynamic, focused on the immediate, creative, courageous, spontaneous, excitable and enthusiastic.

Earth signs are practical, grounded, dependable, materialistic, solid, cautious, conserving and introverted.

Air signs are flexible, communicative, mentally oriented, rational, alert, inventive, objective and co-operative.

Water signs are emotional, feeling, intuitive, sensitive, nurturing, compassionate and receptive.

Quality

The qualities show how the element is expressed through the sign. The cardinal quality is leading and initiating. *Cardinal* signs used to be called *moveable* signs because they mark the change of seasons. They suggest things that alter and last a short time, coming to a quick resolution.

The *fixed* quality is lasting and stable. They suggest situations that endure or drag on and show stability.

Mutable signs used to be called *common* signs because being located between the cardinal and fixed signs, they combine the qualities of both. The mutable quality is adaptable and changeable and show imminent change.

Heat and moisture

Hot signs are in a state of activity whereas cold signs are in a state of rest. Hot signs expend energy and are in a state of motion and cold signs conserve energy and tend to stay the same.

Moist signs are those that are acted upon and are malleable and passive. *Dry* signs are proactive and are solid.

The hot signs are all masculine whereas the cold signs are feminine. Also, the masculine signs are day signs and the feminine signs night signs.

Other groups

Fruitful and *barren* signs are relevant for charts referring to pregnancy or gardening.

Humane signs are concerned with furthering human ideals.

Feral signs are seen as unpredictable and uncontrollable.

Voice

A mute sign rising in a horary chart suggests that there will be little or no news about the matter in question, or that news will be slow in arriving.

	Polarity	Season	Element	Mode	Heat and moisture				Voice
Aries	+	Spring	Fire	Cardinal	Hot and dry				Half
Taurus	-	Spring	Earth	Fixed	Cold and dry				Half
Gemini	+	Spring	Air	Mutable	Hot and moist	Barren	Humane		Loud
Cancer	-	Summer	Water	Cardinal	Cold and moist	Fruitful			Mute
Leo	+	Summer	Fire	Fixed	Hot and dry	Barren	Humane	Feral	Half
Virgo	-	Summer	Earth	Mutable	Cold and dry	Barren			Loud
Libra	+	Autumn	Air	Cardinal	Hot and moist		Humane		Loud
Scorpio	-	Autumn	Water	Fixed	Cold and moist	Fruitful			Mute
Sagittarius	+	Autumn	Fire	Mutable	Hot and dry			Feral, last part of	Half
Capricorn	-	Winter	Earth	Cardinal	Cold and dry				Weak
Aquarius	+	Winter	Air	Fixed	Hot and moist		Humane		Weak
Pisces	-	Winter	Water	Mutable	Cold and moist	Fruitful			Mute

Physical description

In horary astrology the sign that is on the ascendant is descriptive of the querent, or person asking the question. The physical description associated with each of the signs should describe this person. If it does so then your horary chart is a strong one. If it doesn't, the chart may not be as relevant to the issue.

Aries: Ruddy complexion, lean body, long neck, large bones, strong limbs. Males often suffer from baldness or thinning of the hair.

Taurus: Strong, short, well set body, full face, broad forehead, big eyes, large mouth, thick lips, short big hand, black hair, curly or frizzy hair.

Gemini: Slender, young looking, sparkling eyes, long limbed.

Cancer: Short with broad waist and wide neck. Round face and small eyes.

Leo: Tall and large framed with thick, luxuriant hair.

Virgo: Delicate features and an angular but solid build. A slender body, above average middle height; straight or smooth hair rather than curly.

Libra: Fine and pleasing features and good bone structure. Tall, straight, well framed body, slender especially when young. Round, face, bright complexion, pale hair, long and smooth hair, grey or pale eyes.

Scorpio Sturdy with wide shoulders, not very tall. Penetrating eyes, broad face, dull or brown hair, curly or frizzy hair, an hairy body, short necked, strong set body.

Sagittarius: Long, oval face and almond shaped eyes with a strong and able body.

Capricorn: Mean stature, thin and lean face, thin beard, black hair, long small neck, narrow chin. Long limbs, a big boned body and a square jaw.

Aquarius: Tall and slender body with long legs and a lighter complexion than usual. Long face.

Pisces: Short, large face, pale complexion, fleshy body and a tendency to gain weight.

Sickness

Aries: Pimples, harelips, headache, toothache, migraine, baldness, illness or injury to the head or face.

Taurus: Infirmities in the neck and throat.

Gemini: Infirmities in the arms, shoulders and hands. Blood conditions.

Cancer: Conditions of the breast and stomach. Weak digestion, coughs, phlegm.

Leo: Infirmities of the back, ribs and sides, as pains in the back, convulsions, pleurisy, heart conditions, fever, jaundice and sore eyes. Heart, back, sides and ribs.

Virgo: Belly and entrails. Colic, worms, bowel complaints, kidney stones.

Libra: Conditions of the kidneys and bladder, weakness of the back.

Scorpio: Infirmities of the genitals and bladder, piles, conditions of the womb.

Sagittarius: Infirmities in the thighs and buttocks.

Capricorn: Conditions of the knees, itching and scabs.

Aquarius: Infirmities in the legs or ankles, such as gout and cramp. Legs and ankles.

Pisces: Diseases in the feet. Feet.

Professions

Aries: Surgery, armed forces, sports.
Taurus: Chef, gardener, banker, musician.

Gemini: Writer, accountant, salesman, clerk.

Cancer: Caring professions or in those that deal with the public or in antiques.

Leo: Actor, entertainer, agent, hairdresser.

Virgo: Researcher, clerk, cleaner, librarian.

Libra: Fashion and beauty, interior design, antiques, diplomatic corps and modelling.

Scorpio: Detective, researcher, healer, psychologist.

Sagittarius: Law, politics, teaching, PR, advertising.

Capricorn: Government, accountant, estate agent, managerial consultant.

Aquarius: IT, publishing, telecommunications.

Pisces: Film, theatre, caring professions, sailors.

Colour

The colours of the signs can sometimes be useful if, for example, you are searching for a lost object.

Aries	White mixed with red
Taurus	White mixed with lemon
Gemini	White mixed with red
Cancer	Green or russet
Leo	Red or green
Virgo	Black speckled with blue
Libra	Black, dark crimson, or tawny
Scorpio	Brown
Sagittarius	Yellow or green tending to red
Capricorn	Black or russet or a dark brown
Aquarius	Sky colour or blue
Pisces	White glittering colour

Place

Each sign refers to a particular place and direction. This information is needed if you cast a horary chart to find a lost object. It may simply describe the place something is located when you are asking other questions. Signs cusps can be symbolic of boundaries. For example, a significator changing signs may show the missing item is behind something, near a boundary or near the joining of two rooms.

Fire signs indicate places near heat or fire: near chimneys or radiators or where fires have been, near iron or the walls and partitions of a house—or east.

Earth signs indicate places on the ground, under or near the pavement or floor, near mud or clay— or south.

Water signs indicate places near water: bathrooms, kitchens, moist places in the room. In the garden, places near pits, cisterns, ponds, etc—or north.

Air signs indicate places of high elevation or locations with an open view: the upper part of rooms or places near the top of the house, near windows or sources of light. Outside they indicate locations high from the ground, or higher than the ordinary ground; the highest hill or hanging on a tree—or west.

Cardinal signs show high places, lofts, upper rooms, newly erected buildings or newly worked land, hilly countryside. Places where there is a lot of movement or change. The significator of the property in a cardinal sign generally shows that it is not far from its owner.

Fixed signs indicate woods, parks, low places, near the earth, well hidden, or on level ground.

Mutable signs indicate places near water, the eaves of houses, covered places, closets, ante-chambers and rooms within rooms. The significator in a mutable sign can indicate it is inside the home.

Humane signs indicate that the lost object will be found in a place frequented by people—such as the home, rather than outside in a secluded area.

Aries: East. Sandy, dry, hilly grounds, kennel. Baker's, barber's, foundry, sports or club, hardware store, butchers, dentist's. In or near a chimney, heater, stove, room where machinery and tools are kept, garage, toolshed or toolbox, room with locked doors or closets, places where iron or junk is stored, area where guns are kept, under ashtrays, hat boxes, near ceilings, roofs,plastering or doorway.

Taurus: Southeast. Close to the ground or the floor. Low rooms and cellars, places near the earth, outhouses, sheds and stables. Bank, jeweller's, gift shop, carpet shop, loan office or company, dance hall, theatre, clothes shop. Storage room, quiet room that is dimly lit with low ceilings, dark closet, woman's clothes, trunk, cashbox, sage, storage place for furniture, music room, near a piano, chest of drawers, jewellery box, wallet, handbag, suit of clothes.

Gemini: West by south. Chests, high places, panelled rooms, offices and near office or communication equipment. Areas where games are played. Bookshop, bus station, service station, library, train station, subway, school, post office, storehouse, garage, mailbox and office building. Upstairs bedroom, hall, doorway, stairs, study, trunk, chest, desk, briefcase, luggage, room where books are kept, bookshelves.

Cancer: North. Watery places, utility rooms, wash houses, bathrooms, kitchens, cisterns, near a sink or plumbing. Grocer's, bakery, saloon, pub, cafe, public building, restaurant, nursery school, laundrette and reservoir. Dining room, linen closet, pantry, room where articles of sentimental value are kept, room with the most windows, areas where fishing equipment is kept, area where china, silverware or kitchenware is stored.

Leo: West by north. Places where animals frequent. Hard, stony or gravelly ways. Wood, park, playground, magnificent buildings, near the chimney or a source of heat. Casino, betting shop, bar, sports arena, theatre, dance hall, circus, poolroom, government building, golf course, race track. Conservatory, playroom, living room, toybox, children's bedroom.

Virgo: South by west. Garden, where pets are kept, kennel. Doctor's, health spa, vet's, nursing home, dry cleaners, grocer's, accountant's office, pharmacy, zoo, police station, nursery, tenant's place. Cupboard, pantry, bookcase, desk, study, exercise room, filing cabinet, sick person's room, storeroom, study, drawers.

Libra: West. Top of a hill, flower garden, gravel field, close to lawn furniture. Place of entertainment, hotel, theatre, beauty salon, bank, dressmaker's, art gallery, furniture shop, boutique. Upper rooms in houses, lofts, attics and closets, bedroom, dressing room, wardrobe, dressing table, jewellery box, top drawers of a chest, top piece of furniture, broom closet, on a shelf, among your partner's belongings, under a bed, with hobby supplies, attic, guest room.

Scorpio: North by east. In or near a stagnant pool, location subject to flooding, in or near a bin. Butcher's, collection agency, dentist's, public toilet, abandoned house, cesspool, funeral parlour, graveyard, rubbish dump, massage parlour, insurance building, pharmacy. Bathroom, toilet, next to water pipes, dirty part of the house where rubbish is stored, bin, part of the house where it gets rotted or mildewed, room or desk where unpaid bills are kept, empty room, wash room, medicine cabinet, secret drawer or chest, in a hiding place.

Sagittarius: East by south. Hills and high land, on sloping ground. Church, courthouse, betting shop, casino, stable, racing track, college, university, places of public function, solicitor's, bookshop and lecture hall. Upper room, near or in the fireplace or radiator, largest room of the house, places where entertainment of guests is held, men's clothes, room where insurance policies are kept, room where pets are allowed in the house, place where prayer books and college books are stored.

Capricorn: South. In a corner. Places related to livestock or pets, barren and thorny grounds, low rooms in houses, dark places near the ground. Churchyard, graveyard, cemetery, cave, city dump, business place, brick building, police station, funeral parlour, courthouse, parent's home, dark places, abandoned building, place surrounded by fences or close to a fence. Basement, disorderly room, rooms with leather or plastic accessories furnishings, room with old worn furniture, room where an old person stays, garage, near a fridge or freezer, dark places that are hard to reach, shelf where there are ceramics, next to an air conditioner, place where rubbish is kept, places where wood is stored, In a corner, wool objects.

Aquarius: West by north. Hilly and uneven places. High places, the attic, roof, and upper part of all rooms, in or near places recently dug up, uneven ground, in or next to a garage, places where you park your car. Airport, club house, factory, garage, petrol station, motorway, train station, public places, a friend's house. In or near a built-in device or equipment, near electrical appliance, TV room, telephone area, close to a meter or fuse box, close to a light in a room that has been modernised, upstairs, near a draughty window.

Pisces: North by west. Grounds full of water, springs, fishponds, rivers, wells, cisterns, and those places in houses where water is found, bathroom, kitchen, all damp places, rivers, fishponds. Hospital, care home, prison, convent, pub, a dock, drugstore, off licence, fish market, shoe shop, petrol station, asylum, a church. Closet, by a fish tank, wine cellar, bedroom, bathroom, shower, cold or damp floor, medicine cabinet, place where it is hard to access, near glass, near photographic equipment, secret hiding place, hidden inside something, clothes pocket, part of the house where the water comes in.

ASPECTS

Only applying aspects are used (those getting closer) as separating aspects represent things that have already happened. If a retrograde planet is involved, be careful you don't mistake an applying for a separating aspect or vice versa. The closer to exact an aspect is, the stronger it is.

Most modern astrologers assign *orbs* denoting a sphere of influence to aspects, allowing a varying amount of leeway depending on the aspect. However, traditionally an aspect's influence depended entirely on the two planets involved. Each planet radiates a certain amount of light, and that sphere or orb extends a number of degrees in front of and behind the planet. When the orbs of two planets intersect, the aspect is felt.

The way to determine if two planets are in aspect is to add the *moieties* (half-orbs) of the planets together.

For example, the moiety of the Sun is $7\frac{1}{2}°$ and of Saturn is $4°$.

$$7° + 4\frac{1}{2}° = 12°$$

Therefore, if the Sun is at 7° of Cancer and Saturn is at 15° of Cancer, the two planets are in conjunction.

Planet	Orb	Moiety
Sun	15 °	7½°
Moon	12 °	6°
Mercury	7°	3½°
Venus	7°	3½°
Mars	7°	3½°
Jupiter	9°	4½°
Saturn	9°	4½°

The only aspects that matter are the Ptolemaic aspects and conjunction. These are the conjunction (0°, planets in the same sign), opposition (180°, planets in opposing signs), trine (120°, planets in the same element), square (90°, planets in the same modality) and sextile (60°, planets in the same polarity but different elements).

A conjunction, trine or sextile usually gives a positive answer and a square or opposition a negative one.

PERFECTION

Bringing a matter to a resolution is termed *perfection*.

The significators for the querent and the quesited must come together by an applying conjunction or major aspect. This denotes that the matter will come to pass. An aspect is made by the faster of two planets, to the slower. Applying aspects describe what is to come, while separating aspects describe what has already occurred.

Dexter aspect: An aspect made against the order of the signs is stronger.

Sinister aspect: An aspect made with the order of the signs.

Partile: When planets occupy the same degree and make an aspect.

Platic: When two planets are within orb of an aspect but occupy different degrees.

Mutual application: When one planet is retrograde, two planets may apply towards each other in aspect.

Other means of perfection

Sometimes, the significtors don't aspect each other but they have a connection in other ways.

Reception

Mutual reception is when two planets are in each other's dignities. They act as if they were in one another's position. If two planets are in one another's sign they are in mutual reception by rulership. If they are in one another's exaltation, they are in mutual reception by exaltation. If the two planets are in dignities assigned to the other, but the nature of the dignities are different this is called *mixed reception*. (For example, Mars is in Cancer, ruled by the Moon, and the Moon is in Capricorn where Mars is exalted.)

Reception is only relevant if the two planets concerned are also making an aspect to one another. It creates a bond between the two planets and they can be read as if they had exchanged places in the chart. Reception guarantees that the aspect draws the attention of both parties involved, ensuring that its prospects are fully exploited.

Translation of light

A fast moving planet separates from an exact aspect with one planet and then applies to an exact aspect with another planet (these can be separate events). The fast moving planet is said to *transfer the light* between the planet it is separating from and the planet it is applying to. It acts as if it is carrying a message between the two planets concerned.

If the aspects involved are good, the matter will be solved quickly and without difficulty. If the aspects are bad, it will take time and effort. If the first planet receives the translating planet in any of its essential dignities, that ensures an easier flow of events.

Often, the planet translating light is the Moon. As the Moon is also the co-significator for the querent, this shows perfection of the matter.

In the following chart, the Moon has recently made a sextile to Jupiter. It has moved on and will next make a trine to Mercury. Therefore, the Moon has transferred the light from Jupiter to Mercury.

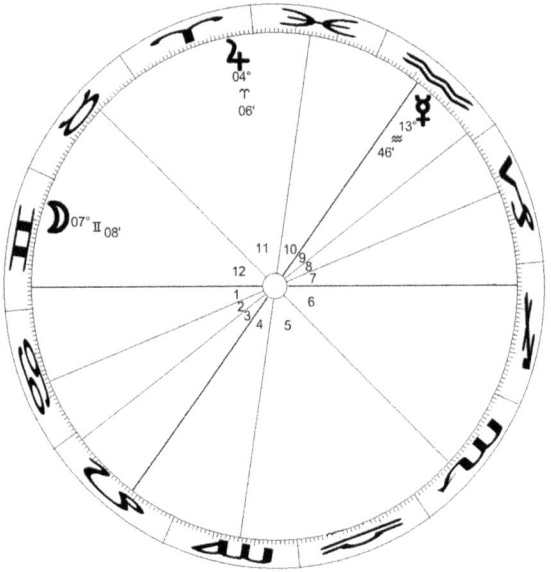

Collection of light

This occurs when two planets (that may or may not make
an aspect to each other) both apply to a third planet that
collects their light and establishes a relationship between
the two. (The slowest planet gets together with two
faster planets.) For example, below the Moon applies
(out of sign) to a square of Jupiter. Mercury applies to
a sextile of Jupiter, which collects the light of the Moon.

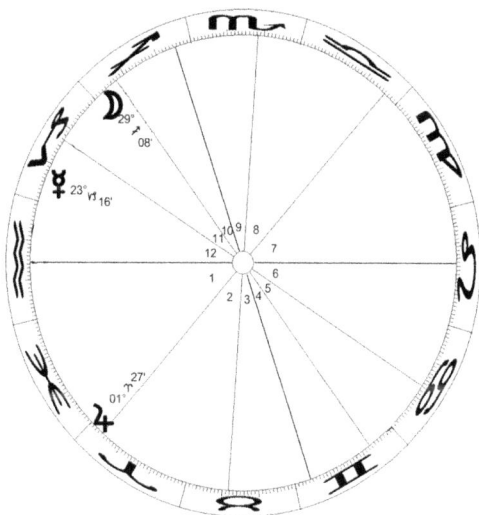

Prohibition

A *prohibition* is something that prevents the matter from reaching a resolution. This isn't always a bad thing as the question may be about something you don't want to happen.

Prohibition

Two significators are directly applying but a third planet standing between them in degrees is closest to the receiving significator. In the chart below before Mercury can reach Jupiter, Mercury makes an opposition to Saturn which prohibits the sextile from being effective.

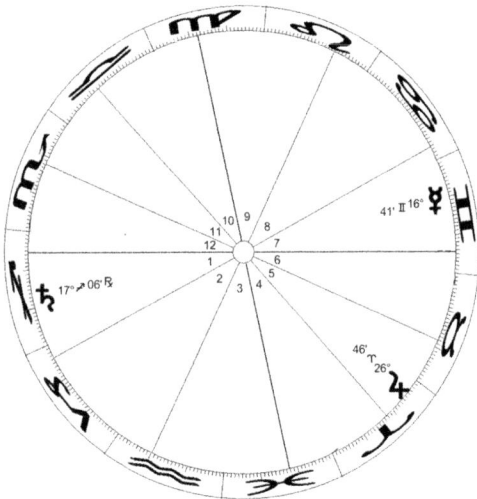

In the chart below the Moon approaches a trine to Jupiter, but before it gets there it sextiles Mars.

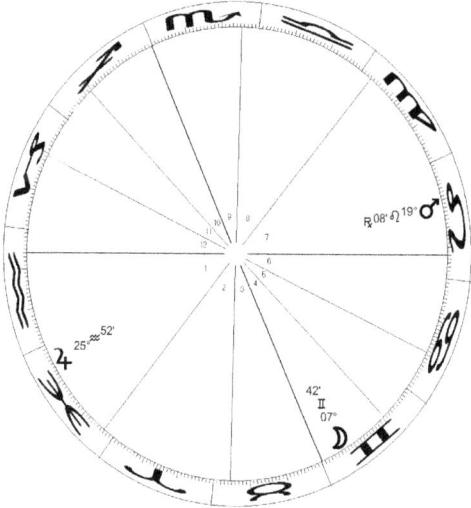

Frustration

One planet applies to aspect another, but before the aspect culminates, a third planet interposes to anticipate the culmination of the forming aspect by completing one of its own. For example, Mercury wants to conjoin Mars but before it gets there Mars conjoins Saturn. Frustration might not prohibit a positive outcome, but tends to show outside interference, the nature of which will be revealed by the interfering planet and the house it rules.

Intervention

When two planets are applying to aspect, but before that aspect can perfect, another planet perfects an aspect first. This mitigates the effects of the applying aspect.

Abscission

Abscission means 'cutting the light' and occurs by either frustration or intervention.

Contrariety

Contrariety is a type of interposition characterised by the contrary or retrograde motion of the interposing planet.

> Mars 10° Scorpio
> Saturn 16° Scorpio
> Jupiter 17° Leo (Rx)

Mars and Saturn are significators applying by conjunction. Jupiter (lighter than Saturn but heavier than Mars) approaching its station before turning retrograde. When it does, it squares Saturn and then Mars before Mars can conjoin Saturn.

Refranation

Two significators are applying by aspect, but before their aspect is perfected, the applying significator turns retrograde and *refrains* from the perfection of the aspect. It can suggest someone backing out of an arrangement.

Evasion

Evasion occurs when two significators are in applying aspect, but before their aspect can be perfected, the receiving significator changes signs, thus evading the perfection and denying the desired outcome.

Venus 22° Cancer
Jupiter 29° Taurus

Before Venus can perfect the sextile with Jupiter, Jupiter evades her by changing sign. Mars is applying to Saturn but before it gets there, Saturn is in the next sign.

Retrograde

If the significator is retrograde, it places the querent in a weak position. If the two significators are both retrograde, it suggests the matter may not come to fruition.

Combustion

If a significator is within 8½° of the Sun (but more than 17 minutes away), it is said to be combust and this suggests a negative outcome.

Return of light

When a planet applies to another planet, the applying one sends out its light to be received by the other. Return of light occurs when one of the significators is either retrograde or combust.

Mars 10° Gemini
Jupiter 12° Leo
Sun 19° Leo

Mars and Jupiter are significators. Mars applies to Jupiter and sends out its light to him. However, Jupiter is weakened by combustion and returns the light of Mars to Mars.

TIMING

There are a number of ways of assessing when something indicated by the horary chart is likely to happen.

Each question carries its own time-frame with a short, medium and long possibility. For example, days, weeks and months. The units follow each other, so you don't have (for example) minutes, months and years. The context of the question will usually indicate the units, which may be:

Minutes, hours, days
Hours, days, weeks
Days, weeks, months
Weeks, months, years

For example, if Mercury is at 8° applying to Mars at 12° and the ephemeris shows that the aspect perfects when they are both at 16° of their signs, Mercury has had to travel 8° to perfect the aspect. Therefore, the event will occur in 8 units. Looking in the ephemeris is always useful because you can check that a planet doesn't go retrograde before the aspect completes.

Alternatively, you can assume that Mars stands still and take only the distance between the planets' positions, which in this instance is 4° and so it will take 4 units. This is the most common method and the easiest.

If the planet's daily motion at the time of the question is slower than average, this will cause delay or extend the time period. A fast moving planet will speed things up.

If the aspect is to a retrograde planet, the event can happen faster than the number of degrees suggests.

The Moon indicates change so the degrees from the Moon to an exact aspect with the significator; the number of degrees separating the Moon from an exact applying aspect with the significator; the number of degrees that separate the Moon or the significator from one of the angles or the number of degrees that separate the Moon or the significator from the end of the sign they are in may give the answer.

Another possibility is the number of degrees between a 1st house planet to the ruler of the house which represents the question.

If there are two aspects indicating the event will happen, they may show the same time but different units. For example, if one shows 12 units and the other 3, this could represent 12 weeks or 3 months.

To decide which time unit to choose, you need to consider the sign and the house in which the applying planet stands, ignoring the sign and house in which the planet applied to stands.

Fixed signs give the longest time-unit, cardinal the shortest and mutable the middle.

Angular houses by nature give the slowest time unit, cadent the fastest and succedent the middle. However, a planet in an angular house has a lot of accidental dignity and so an increased power to act. Therefore, angular houses are fast if the planet in an angular house is in a position to act.

For example, if you are waiting for a parcel to arrive, as the parcel can't do anything to speed up its arrival the angular house suggests a slow time unit. However, if the question is about starting a relationship, the querent can do something about the situation and therefore the planet signifying them being placed in an angular house suggests a fast time unit.

Combining the house and sign gives a combination of units. Long and long gives the longest unit. Short and short gives the shortest. Any other combination gives the middle unit.

If while applying to a significator the Moon changes sign or house, refer to the original sign and house and don't attempt to combine time units.

Timing can be complicated and need only be used if the question itself includes it.

SPECIFIC QUESTIONS

Relationships

Relationship questions are probably the most common horary questions you will be asked. The same rules apply whatever the nature of the relationship.

The querent is represented by the 1st house, its ruler and the Moon.

The other person is shown by the 7th house and its ruler.

Any planets in these houses can be considered as co-significators, especially if located near the cusp. They often describe the people involved.

The Sun is also a general significator for the man and Venus a general significator for the woman. This is particularly useful when the Moon represents one of the people involved.

In addition, the Moon is the natural significator of wives; Venus sweethearts; Mars young men; Sun men of confidence and Saturn mature or older men.

The 5th house is the house of love affairs and if the Moon or a significator falls in the 5th house, it suggests heightened passion but not necessarily a long term commitment.

A good aspect between the ruler of the 1st house and the ruler of the 7th shows a willingness to form a union. This is strengthened if there is also reception. When there is no applying aspect, translation or collection of light can achieve the same result, suggesting the assistance of a third party.

If the application or translation is by square or opposition without reception, a good result is unlikely. A relationship is possible if there is reception, but the situation is difficult and there will be obstacles. If the application is frustrated by the interception of another planet, or by one of the significators turning retrograde, the relationship will be broken off or hindered by someone or a situation symbolised by the interposing planet.

The fastest moving significator shows the one who is most enthusiastic about the relationship. Similarly, the 1st house ruler in the 7th house suggests the querent is the most enthusiastic, and the 7th house ruler in the 1st shows opposite.

An application from the Sun or Moon to Venus, assuming both are well placed and strong, suggests the relationship will develop.

Lost objects

The querent is symbolised by the ascendant, its ruler, and the Moon. (The Moon is also a natural significator for anything lost.)

All moveable possessions (no matter what their size is) are signified by the 2nd house and its ruler.

You also need to consider the natural significator for the lost object. For example:

Sun: valuable things; gemstones; articles made of or coloured gold.

Moon: glassware; crockery; pearls; mirror; pale or white things; items made of silver; antiques.

Mercury: documents; books; magazines; passports; coins; tickets.

Venus: ornaments; jewelry; clothes; handbags; make-up.

Mars: knives; machinery; tools; red objects.

Jupiter: religious artifacts; items connected with wealth (bank books); legal items.

Saturn: objects made of leather; old things, dark or heavy things.

Similarly, the ruler of the house associated with the object may offer useful information. For example, the 3rd house ruler for a document.

The sign on the cusp of the 4th house and its ruler help to describe where the item is and the quality of ground it is on.

Whether or not the item will be found is shown by the strength of the significator of the missing object or a positive connection between the significator of the querent and the lost object lost. Without such a connection, recovery is unlikely.

Finding the object is more likely if:

The Moon is: angular; the ruler of the 2nd house, ascendant, ruler of the ascendant, Jupiter, Venus, Fortuna or the North Node; is placed in the ascendant, 2nd or 4th house; applying to the ascendant or its ruler; applying to the 2nd house ruler, a planet in the 2nd house or to Fortuna; applying to its own dispositor. The Moon aspecting a fortune shows the item is in the safe keeping of someone who will return it.

The Sun and Moon are: aspecting each other or the cusp of the 2nd house by trine; aspecting each other by any aspect out of angles.

The Sun is: in the ascendant (unless in Libra or Aquarius); the ruler of the 2nd house.

The ruler of the 2nd house is angular. If it is in the 10th or 11th house, that shows that the object is near the querent or held by a friend.

Finding the object is unlikely if:

Both the Sun and Moon are under the Earth (in the 1st, 2nd, 3rd, 4th, 5th, or 6th house).

The Moon is: in a cadent house; far from the querent's significator; in the 7th or 8th house aspected by the ruler of the 7th (suggesting theft); under Sun's beams (between 8½° and 17° from the Sun); combust (17 minutes and 8½° from the Sun), in the 8th house; applying to the 8th house ruler; separating from its own dispositor; aspecting an infortune (Mars, Saturn, South Node); disposed of by an infortune.

The ruler of the 2nd house is: in a cadent house; far from the querent's significator; in the 7th or 8th house aspected by the ruler of the 7th (suggesting theft); under Sun's beams (between 8½° and 17° from the Sun); combust (17 minutes and 8½° from the Sun), in the 8th house; applying to the 8th house ruler; separating from its own dispositor; aspecting an infortune (Mars, Saturn, South Node); disposed of by an infortune.

An infortune (Mars, Saturn, South Node) is in the ascendant or 2nd house.

To work out when an object may be found, look at the aspect between the two planets signifying recovery.

How the item was lost is shown by the last aspect of the ascendant ruler. If it separates from:

Sun: by means of a person of authority.
Moon: through frequent, everyday use, or by means of a messenger or mature woman.
Mars: through fear or anger.
Mercury: through a connection with writing or messages.
Venus: through drinking, gambling, play, or a young woman.
Jupiter: due to an excess of care or a reorganisation of household affairs.
Saturn: due to forgetfulness.

To find out where a lost object is, consider the:

Sign on the ascendant and its ruler
Sign on the 2nd cusp and its ruler
Sign on the 4th cusp and its ruler
Moon's sign
Fortuna's sign

If the Moon or 2nd house ruler is within 30° of the ruler of the ascendant, the object is at home or near the querent.

If the 2nd house ruler is in the ascendant or in the same sign as the ruler of the ascendant, or in one of the signs it rules, it is where the querent spends most time.

The 10th house shows the place of work, the 7th house the property of a partner, the 4th house the oldest part of the home, property belonging to the querent's father, or somewhere that old people spend their time.

Legal matters

Querent: 1st house, ruler, Moon
Opponent: 7th house, ruler
Judge: 10th house, ruler
Verdict: 4th house, ruler

The 2nd house shows the querent's money, lawyers and witnesses (those acting on their behalf).

The 8th house is the opposition's money.

The ruler of the 11th house shows if the querent is likely to get what they want.

The dignities of the rulers of the 1st and 7th houses show the integrity of the parties.

Receptions can show how each side feels about the other. The planet that signifies the querent has high regard for their opponent if that planet is in the exaltation of the planet that rules the opponent and vice versa. This suggests a possible settlement.

Contests and sports

This issue with sports horaries is that the question of who will win is likely to be asked by a large number of people at different times. When the sport involves a league, the question of who will be the outright winner may be asked numerous times over several months. However, some people have had success with sports horaries so the basic rules appear below.

When it is a straightforward win or lose situation, the team that begins the match is represented by the ascendant, its ruler and any planets in the first house and the challenging team by the seventh house, its ruler and any planets in the seventh house. In most sports, the challenging team is the away team.

In the World Cup, the matches are played in one country and so there is only one true home team. However, the team that wins the toss begins play and so is signified by the first house.

Choosing the winning team

For the ascendant team to win, the ascendant ruler should be strong and Venus or Jupiter in the first house (or be the ascendant ruler) and not retrograde.

If the Moon is near the ascendant or midheaven, the ascendant team will win.

If the Moon is near the seventh or fourth house cusp, the seventh house team will win.

If the ascendant ruler is on the descendant, the ascendant team will win (and vice versa).

If the North Node is in the first house, this bodes well for the ascendant team (and vice versa).

A ruler in an angular house is stronger than a ruler in a cadent or succedent house.

The closer a ruler is to a house cusp, the greater its effect on that house. If a ruler is in a different sign to the house cusp, its effect is diminished.

The Moon aspecting the ruler of the ascendant suggests that the ascendant team has the advantage (and vice versa). The ruler the Moon last aspected is more likely to win, especially if the aspect is a conjunction.

If the Moon conjoins, sextiles or trines the Part of Fortune, the ascendant team will win (vice versa for a square or opposition).

If the Part of Fortune conjoins the North Node, the ascendant team will win (and vice versa).

When the Moon is in the via combusta, the outcome is unpredictable.

If the ruler of the ascendant is retrograde or otherwise debilitated, the ascendant team will lose (and vice versa).

If the ruler of the ascendant or the Moon is afflicted or debilitated, the ascendant team will lose. If the ruler of the descendant is afflicted or debilitated, the opposing team will lose.

Draw

A match is usually a draw if the Moon:

Is in detriment or fall

Applies to a malefic

Is combust

Has a combust dispositor

Applies to or separates from a conjunction of the South node

Has a dispositor that applies to or separates from a conjunction of the South node

Has a retrograde dispositor

Is void of course (give unpredictable results)

Additionally, a draw can be indicated if the planetary is immediately about to change or has just changed (within minutes).

Extra time and penalties

When the angles, their rulers and the Moon are cardinal, the match will complete within its time.

When the angles, their rulers and the Moon are mutable, extra time may be expected.

When the angles, their rulers and the Moon are fixed, this slows things down and penalties can be expected.

Holding a title

When one team holds a trophy or a title and must be beaten in order to lose that it and where a draw means the trophy stays with the holder, the holder is signified by the 4th house and the challenger by the ascendant.